POST

Andrew Fry

Dedicated to my late

Uncle David Morrish

PROFILE

Andrew was Born in 1961.
He has lived most of His Life in North Devon.
His interests are Theatre, Poetry of World War One, together with The American Civil War and watching Football, as a big Fan of Tottenham Hotspur.
Andrew was also a founding member of the Barnstaple Writers', which continues to meet at the Barnstaple Library.

Although He has Cerebral Palsy, this did not prevent him from marrying Jean in 1993,
Who had Graduated from Moorlands College in the Summer of 1985. Over the years Andrew has written and campaigned with Jean on many Disability Issues. Working as he has done, first as an Office Clerk and then as a Historical Researcher. Since then Andrew and Jean have been involved with a Counselling Organization and different Church activities.

As Andrew is Politically aware believing as he does in Social Justice, he became part of The Christian Socialist Movement, as well as joining The National Poetry Society, The South West Disability Development Arts Agency and North Devon Arts.

Along side this, he has found time to attend The Way with Words Literature Festival, near Totnes. As well as gaining a small bursary from the South West Arts in order to attend Totleigh Barton Devon, this took place in the late Summer of 1988, where Andrew was tutored by John Moat and John Fairfax.

In 2010 Andrew was asked if he would take part for the first time in the North Devon "Theatre Fest" which takes place during the 30 days of June. It was also during this time he exhibited some of his Poetry.

In 2012 Andrew and Jean took a rescue Cat on by the name of Star. She is now twelve. Since then although suffering much illness, including a seventeen day hospital visit.

During July 2015 Andrew was invited to the first R.H.S. Rosemoor's Literary Day, and from this later attended the Appledore Book Festival.

In 2018 he began volunteering at the Barnstaple Museum found at the Square, Barnstaple. During the opening year of refurbishment he has become their Poet in Residence. It is because of this Artefacts and Curiosities came about, during the Autumn of two thousand and nineteen. Since this Andrew has Published with Amazon two more volumes of Poetry, they are "Hidden Paths" and "Moor Poetry" concerning Dartmoor and Exmoor. He now writes "Petra Car Ea", a celebration of his Sixty years, upon God's Good Earth.

4

Andrew continues to write both Poetry and Prose and sincerely believes that we are here to imitate our Father, the Creator. As we continue to Carol through the colours of all our lives. Travelling as Andrew does extensively through Europe and the Middle East.

His titles are Petra Car Ea, Clouds and Clouds, Marionette, Breaking Chains, Taw Poems as well as Just Passing, most recently The Golden Hare, and Hand me Down my Walking Cane, Greystone Memories, Graffiti Poem, Down Paternoster Row and Voice, as well as of course Artefacts and Curiosities which can be found on Amazon along with Andrew's Early Works.

CONTENTS

p.11 Coronation Poem
p.12 Albion Street
p.13 Unicorns and Kings
p.15 Men in Sheds
p.16 Possibilities
p.17 And Michael Walks
p.18 I am not a Jerk!
p.19 Public Rant, Society needs to change, Not I
p.20 Spastic Claw
p.21 Excluded
p.22 The Lame Man Walks
p.23 Epilepsy
p.24 I've lived to tell the tale
p.25 Wonderland
p.26 Raven Bird
p.27 The Peacock Eyes
p.28 Coughs and Sneezes, and Winter Breezes
p.30 When Tears Fall
p.31 Quake!
p.33 Take a Moment
p.35 Elegy to David
p.36 One more Forgotten Hero
p.37 Farewell to the Old Works
p.39 Ken
p.41 Dad
p.42 Last Kiss
p.43 She
p.44 Sirius
p.45 The Leaving of our Joy

p.46 Billy Boy
p.48 Green
p.49 The Trouble with Old Goliath my Dear
p.50 Jerusalem in the Morning
p.52 Good Friday Poem
p.53 The Cross
p.54 A Curse Conceived
p.55 Jesus Christ
p.56 Derelict Man
p.57 War is Over
p.58 Purple Friday
p.59 The Chapel in the Rock
p.61 Touch Stone Poem
p.62 And God Came Down to Earth One Day
p.63 A Take on the Nativity
p.64 Holy Saturday
p.66 Risen
p.67 Have You seen the Lion?
p.68 A Season of Optimism and Joy
p.70 Four Letters
p.71 The Sun
p.72 Boscastle
p.73 Worth
p.74 Mariupol
p.75 Butter Fly Bombs
p.76 Russia the Great Bear
p.77 The Naked Lady
p.78 To Pray as You Go
p.79 Turning the Tide
p.81 Admiral
p.82 Oh Poor Venice

p.84   The Old Grey Pot
p.86   The Girl
p.87   The Missing Piece
p.88   Uniform
p.89   Who?
p.90   Actor
p.91   Floyd
p.93   The Refugee
p.94   Never
p.95   Migrants
p.96   African Man
p.97   Public Limited Company
p.98   Hands of Time
p.99   Oh Mother of Mine
p.100   The Colours
p.101   Words, the Blood that Runs through My Veins
p.102   Flotsam 'n' Jetsam
p.103   Water
p.104   Constant
p.105   Autumnal Woodland
p.107   The Beginning of Us!
p.108   Those Family Christmases
p.109   Louise
p.110   Nathan the Noise
p.111   Twins
p.113   Sadness in the Margins
p.114   Oh The Kids To Day
p.117   The Old Crow
p.118   In the Arrival
p.120   Oxford
p.121   67

p.122 A Most Passive Lot
p.124 Taw Vale, and Return
p.126 Have You
p.127 Women
p.128 Shadow Fly
p.129 Red Sentinel
p.131 Somers Fall
p.132 78 Days
p.133 Old Peat
p.134 Sketching Ole Stick Jaw
p.137 Along the Granite Way
p.140 Archimedes Pump
p.141 The Tale of Poor Wilfred
p.144 At the Church of My Fore Fathers
p.146 Greystone Memories
p.148 Spirits Having Flown
p.151 The Wealth of a Dartmoor Village
p.154 The Magic of a Dartmoor Scene
p.156 Mine Eyes to Sea
p.158 Cateract
p.159 Taw Boy
p.162 Men at Their Benches
p.164 The Old Works Hooter
p.166 My Wireless
p.167 Worthy Farm
p.169 Flowers
p.170 Satan's Approach
p.172 Rose Hill Children's Hospital
p.174 The Children's Ward
p.175 Children of the Terrace
p.177 Turning Days

p.178 The Central Belt
p.179 89
p.180 Brush Strokes
p.181 The Blue Planet
p.183 Autumns Mill Side Wander
p.185 Beyond the Sallow Tree
p.187 Lament on March 27th
p.188 A Poem for Mothering Sunday
p.189 Mourning Scene
p.190 The Black Madonna
p.191 Albatross
p.192 Street Death
p.193 Pictures and Paintings
p.194 Bedowin's a People Beyond
p.196 Cleave Terrace
p.198 Mr. Nicholas Our Geography Teacher
p.199 Point of Contact
p.200 Coming Home
p.202 History Avenue
p.203 Gold Dust
p.204 Farewell
p.205 Full Stop
p.206 Post

CORONATION POEM

A Crown For A King,
        Charles,

Is Anointed,
Being Defender Of Faiths,
Of Albion Street,
A Most Bejewelled And Septic Of Isles,
Sitting In Glorious Majesty,

When A Nation Parties,
Celebrating,
This Most Ancient Of Realms,
Of Unicorns And Kings.

                                  King Charles Third
                                    May 6th, 2023

ALBION STREET

Have you seen Albion Street?
Where the Cobbles are black,
And the Red Coated Knights are Old,
With Unicorn and Lion Told,

Have you seen Albion Street?
Where the Markets and Memories,
                           Are a-Bustle,

With Myth,
And Freedoms they Make,
To their Music and Yarns they Seek,

Have you seen Albion Street?
Its Pastures Green,
And Chimney's Tall,
Telling of a Different Scene,
Do Watery Canals,
And Engines of Rail,

Have you seen Albion Street?
To Children Small,
Of Chapel,
Learning of Jerusalem,
And Empire Ball,
Being as this many Layered,
                           Onion.

UNICORNS AND KINGS

Shrouded,
Chapels then Steeples,
Bells,
Lessons learnt,
On Slates of Grey,
Of Whittington Hill,
And Empire Day,

Unicorns and Kings,
Stones in the Scape,
Ancient Stones,
Touch Stones,

Arthur he Sleeps,
Forgotten By We,
Down Albion Street,
Tells of Empire Day,
Of White Horses,
Mountains 'n' River,
        Song,

Tell of Old John Barley Corn,
And his Friend the Ferrier,
Striking the Anvil Sound,
When Factory Chimney,
Speaks of Works Day Done,
    At the Old Pit Head,

Singing,

Knowing Men Shall Go To The Front,
Carried By Those Dragons of Steam,
From Our Albion Street.

MEN IN SHEDS

Oh Do You Know That There's Funny Little Men In Sheds?
Potty Little Sheds,
Some May Even Say,
Potty Little Men In Sheds,
Making All Kinds Of Things,
And Tuff,
Yes Making All Manner Of Things,
With Cross Cut,
Grease Gun,
And Lathe,
Whilst Turning The Screw,
Behind Closed Doors,
          There,

In Camera,
With Their Tea,
Their Precious Cup Of Rosie Lee,
Whilst Lingering Away The Hours Spent,
Away From Their Women,
The Female Kind,
Behind Closed Doors,
In A World Of Their Own,
Doing Man Things,
Simply Man Things,
Finding Peace,
Perfect Peace!!

POSSIBILITIES

Writing Is,

    Just Words,
It's Only Words,
Possibilities,
To A Another World,
Through The Window,
Through The Door,
Turn The Key,
And You Shall See,
When Turning A Page,
One Fertile Imagination,
In Colour,
Brought To Life,

        Possibilities!

AND MICHAEL WALKS

Night time,
Is Cedar time,
When Michael walks,
With sticks,
Of white,
Like a blind Man,
With His canes,
Does Martin,
In the Sands of Time
          Play,
          Play,
Masking it,

For the Night is dark,
And the Love Howl,
Hoots,
Hoots r way.

I AM NOT A JERK!

I AM Not A JERK!

I Have cp.

PUBLIC RANT, SOCIETY NEEDS TO CHANGE, NOT I.

Society Needs To Change, Not I,
Do I Have To Travel To Manchester,
Birmingham,
The Isle Of Wight,
Or Even Flaming Glasgow,
Not To Be Crippled,
As You Say,
For You Make Me Disabled,

In What Think,
In How You React,
I see it In Your Face,
You Don't Even Try To Hide It,

The Thing Is,
I am Not Funking Well Handicapped,
But Time And Again,
You Make Me Bloody Well Disabled,
And The Thing Is,
I Call You Friend!

SPASTIC CLAW

Spastic Claw in Winter,
Feels no Pain,
Crow Foot,
And Broad Foot,
Beneath the Tree,
A Gallows Tree,
That Swings,
Swings,
There,
    Oh There Again,
        Again,

When Smearing ones Blood,
Sacred Blood,
Of Easter Holy,
Is that Pain,
In Glory?
Spilt- Then,
Suffers,
Me,
Oh Me!!

EXCLUDED

I am One In Twelve Million,
Here In London Town,
There's A Bus,
A Big Red Bus.
Its A Double Decker London Bus,
And I Wish To Ride,
This Big Red Bus,
Public Bus,
With My Ticket To Ride,
Though I've Chained Myself To The Rawlings,
For I am Excluded,
To Ride This Big Red Bus,
With My Wheels,
For My World,

Have You Ever Tried To Ride The Underground?
In A Chair,
Such As This,
A Wheel Chair!

THE LAME MAN WALKS

The Lame Man
         Walks,

With Casts,

The Lame Man
         Walks,

Wearing his Brace,

The Lame Man
         Walks,

Tasting Bitter Herbs,
His Poetry to Perform.

EPILEPSY

Epilepsy,
And Me,
      Is a Breakfast!

I'VE LIVED TO TELL THE TALE

I am In My Sixties Now,
And My Life Shows It,
At Least Though I've Lived To Tell The Tale!

WONDERLAND

Wonderland Is,
Kids On The Corner,
With Ice Upon Their Noses,
All Wrapped Up Warm,
As Snug As A Bug In A Rug,
Against Those Winter Elements,
Like Their Coal Eyed Cheerful Snowman,
Having To His Topper,
And Carrot Nose,

He Dreamed A Dream,
Of The Bleak Midwinter,
Of Kings,
And Sleigh Bells In The Snow,
When Singing Carols At The Door,
Mother Would Baste The Bird,
Just As Father Settled Himself,
For The Queens Speech!

RAVEN BIRD

Cold Winds Blow,
Cloud over the Sun,
Raven Bird,
Squawks,

19,
Covid - 19,

Pestilence Came,
To the Soulless,
      Street!

THE PEACOCKS EYES

Famine,
And Disease,
Separates,
In the Wilderness,
Family from Neighbour,
Strutting,
Does Covid-19,
Like a Peacock,
Displaying his Eyes,
Around the Village.

COUGHS AND SNEEZES, AND WINTER BREEZES
(A Lament Concerning THE N. H. S.)

Beech Leaves,
And Trees,
Scamper,
Scamper,
In The Wind,
The Wind,
Running,
Chasing Tales,
In This Winter Of Descent,
Of Strikes,
And Yet More Bleadin' Strikes,

For I'm All Of A Cough,
And A-Sneeze,
With Covid,
And The Flu,
Covid,
And The Flu,
Father,
Like You,

So All I'll Do,
Is Rape Up Warm,
In Bed,
For That Thing,
We Call Our Jewel,
In The Crown,
The N. H. S. Is Over Welled,

Over Welled,
So We're Lead To Believe,
             Father!

                    Winter Strikes 2023

WHEN TEARS FALL

When Tears Fall,

    Is Learning To Let Go,
   Of Grief,
   A Grief Observed,
   I Guess,
   When Wrestling,
   That Dark Angel,
And Go On,
        On,

   With Life,
    Life It Self,
      It Self,

Like Poets Speak Now,
        O f A River,

Darling!!

QUAKE!

Gaia!

Shouted 'n' Shock,
And Ached,
In Pain,
At Point Of Birth,
    Was She,
     Was She,

For The Ground Did Rumble,
And Sway,
Nearing Gods Wrath,
At End Day,

Top-ling Offices,
Clasping,
Homes,
And Hospitals,
There Was She,

At Point At Point Of Birth,
Devi -stating All Who Slept,
For Lingering Hours,
    All Day,
    All Day,

To Point Of Earth,
She Shaked Like Hell,

Entombing,
Entombing,

At Point Of Death,
All In Concrete And Clay,
    In Concrete And Clay!

                              Turkey February 2023

TAKE A MOMENT

Oh Look At The Leaves,
The Coloured Leaves,
Of Autumns Haze,
Brush Over Your Shoes,
Then Paint Them,
          Then,

Oh See The Squirrel,
Gathering Nuts,
As He May,
At Play,

Then Take A Moment,
On Your Front Step,
See The Birds On The Wire,
For There's A Song About That,

Then Taste Your Coffee,
Before The Reality Of The Day,
                    Kicks In,

Then Take A moment,
Pray,
Go Explore A Book,
Turn Chapter 'n' Verse,
And See A New World,
Open Unto You,

Listen Then To Your Friend,

With Dull Set Tones,
The Wireless,
Paint Oh So Vivid Pictures,
In Your Mind,

And Be Happy,
When Fishing,
Muse Upon That Cigar,
With Your Piece Of Cheese 'n' Port,
In Your Moment,
Whilst Watching The Waters Of Life,
                        Carry You By,
                        Oh So Sweetly!

ELEGY TO DAVID

Sadly,
Suddenly,
Death Came,
To A Family,
Unexpectedly,

If Death Can Come,
Unexpectedly,
At Ninety Six?

For He Was Part Of The Furniture,
                An Institution,
                Was David.
The Chancellor,
A Soldier,
A Orderly,
A Music Man,

And Then Nearing The End,
He Swooped,
His Military Number,
For The Uniform,
Of The Blood And Thunder,
Did This Christian Soldier,

For When David Was Found,
Oh Then We Knew,
It Was An End Of Era.
                David Morrish, Uncle, Dies 96 Jan 23

ONE MORE FORGOTTEN HERO

Wrapped Against The Cool,
Beneath The Bay Window,
A Form Of A Being,
Lay On Cotton Sheets,
And Cobbles,
In The Alleys,
Away From Prying Eyes,
And Societies Gazes,
Out Of Sight,
Was Out Of Mind,

Whilst A Soldier,
Sold His War Cry,
And Folks Made Way For Christmas,
This Winters Day,
For The Lights Would Be Go On,
To Brighten The Christmas Gloom,
Lights Across High Street,
And Avenue,
Windows To Would Have Their Displays,
As Music Was Sounded,
So To Would People Listen,

Although As For Our Rough Sleeper,
Well He Just Could Have Been,
On More Forgotten Hero?
In A World That Simply Doesn't Care!

FAREWELL TO THE OLD WORKS

I Never Did Feel Regret,
To The Old Works,
With Its Chimney And Whistle,
And Clocks,
Beside The Tide Of The River Flowing,
On Into Tomorrow,
It To Stuck Me as if that Too,
Was Telling The Time,
Slowly Slipping Away,
Into Yesterday.

For I Never Did Feel Regret,
To Leave The Old Works,
It To Me Was Just A Smelly Ole Place
                              Anyway,

For I Would Leave The Old Works,
And Travel Far,
Into That New Morning,
Things Would Be Mine To Do,
Mine To Clutch Hold Of,
And Ascend The Mountain,
                Before Me,

Into That New Morning,
For I Would Write As Well As Travel,
And Writing Was Just Like Perlocution,
In That New Morning,
So I Thought,

For Little Did I know,
That It To Would Take Me That Time,
Time Running By,
On The Taw,
The Taw!

> Written On Leaving
> Shaplands
> 1978-85

KEN

This is to Ken,
The Stickler,
The Brethren Teacher,
Who gave no quarter,
And told no lie,
Telling nothing else,
Of his Church,
The Grosvenor Church,

Whilst laughing little,
He gave a lot,
Out from his Puritan Heart,
To the Boys that he taught,
Carrying a Bible,
A Brethren Bible so Black,

For out and around Barum town he strolled,
A Peaceful Town,
Marching at pace,
He would often say, "can't stop"
But indeed, he did stop,
                    "Dead"

Knowing his Truth,
And there he was laid to his rest,
To join,
All manner of Catholic,
And Protestant Folk,
Awaiting his Lord in the Air!

The Air!

Ken Morrish Died May 23th 2017

DAD

Dad you taught me to walk,
                   To walk,

Alongside Soldiers that marched,
In Tunic's Red,
In Tunic's Red,
With mirrored feet,
And Bear Skin black,
Do they shine,

You taught me to walk,
    Taught me to walk,

First by the left,
And then the right,
Marching,
Marching,
Up Windsor Great Hill,
Like Soldiers on Parade,
Like Soldiers on Parade,

Dad you taught me to Walk,
                   To walk,

You did!
You did!
All that time ago,
      Time ago!

LAST KISS
(A Mother's Kiss - Leaving Harbour)

When Did She last Kiss me?
In the Car Park,
She last Kissed me,
So long, long, ago,
In the Days of Wine,
        And Roses,

She Kissed me,
The Piano Plays,
Now She Sits,
With quiet Hands,
And Distant Eye,
Backward Stepping,

When Did She last Kiss me,
In the Car Park,
She Kissed me,
So long, long, ago.
The Piano Plays.

        This Took Place at a Garden Centre

SHE
(The Problem With Alzheimer's)

She Is a Shroud,
Of Her Former Self,
Whilst Just Being There,
For It Is True To say,
That I Lost My Mother,
Sometime Ago,

For It Is Said,
That It Is Like a Second Bereavement,
And So She Is a Shroud,
Of Her Former Self,
Whilst Just Being There,
At Room Twenty One,
        Not Out,

Locked Into Self,
In Bed,
In Chair,
And I For One,
Keep Asking WHY?
Being Cerebral Of Mind,

To What End,
Is This Purpose?
To Be Locked Into Self,
At Room Twenty One,
        Not Out!

SIRIUS

Mother's under the Apple Tree,
Under The Apple Tree,
Is Mother,

Saying Farewell,
Saying Adieu,
Kissing Her Memories,
Goodbye,
Goodbye,

Beneath such
Stars as
Sirius,

Majoring more often than
Not,
On Her Life,

As a Shadow Casts,
So The Dice has rolled,
In Favour,
Of
Sirius,
Sirius,

My Lovely,
Oh That Star Of Fucking Madness,
Now, You Dog!

                                      When Dementia Hits

THE LEAVING OF OUR JOY
(A Journey Into Dementia)

Oh What Is The Purpose?
And Where Have You Gone?
On This Your Dark Journey,
For I Don't Know,
Slipping Away Through The Night,
               And The Mist,

Was The Leaving Of Joy,
To Take Your Music,
      Of Happiness,

So Rare,
So Rare!

BILLY BOY

Nearing Christmas,
I Heard A Voice,
To The Left Of Me,
Calling My Name,
Calling My Name,

Then Out Of The Darkness,
He Stepped,
The Darkness Of That Chill Winters Eve,
Did Young Billy Boy,

We Had Been To School Together,
But I hadn't See him About,
That Much,
Although I Knew His Life Had Been A Bit Of A Wasted
                                                    One,

That Was True Enough,
When We Stood As Old Mates,
In The Sleight,
Sharing Young Billy Boys Chips,

It Was Then He Asked Me,
How Do You Cope?
Get A Dentist?
A Doctor?
For Billy Had Always Been In,
And Out,
Yo-yoing,

Away,
As He Put It
Just Away To Often!

                                                  A Chance Meeting

GREEN

Green is the Source of Life,
Green are our Woods,
Green is the Camomile Lawn,
        Beneath our Toes,

Then why Pave with Concrete 'n' Clay?

THE TROUBLE WITH OLD GOLIATH MY DEAR

You May Chop Goliaths Head Off,
But It Shall Only Reappear Else Where,
                            Dear David,

For I Fear He Is Nothing But A Many Headed
                                Creature My Love,

Ugly As In Revelation,
                Dear.

JERUSALEM IN THE MORNING

Have you seen Jerusalem in the Morning?
Where the sun rises stirring the hearts of the
 Protagonist
Like dogs in the Deserts,

Have you seen Bethlehem's stall?
Where there's no Star 'n' Straw at all,

Have you seen the Jordan?
Heard the Voice, and seen the Dove,
                              Descending.

Have you Climbed the Mountain,
And been in the Valley Trodden low.

Have you broke bread?
Only to see your Betrayer Come.

Have you felt the nails pierce?
A Carpenter's hands that healed.

Have you seen the Stone rolled away?
Knowing the Captives are free,

Have you met with your Master and Lord, Jesus?
The Christ,
Upon the Emmaus Road,
Then cast your Net wide,
Follow Him,

And Bring the Harvest in.

> Written In Jerusalem After a Visit, Nov 1990
> First Published in Taw Poems, 2000

GOOD FRIDAY POEM

Bolted Nail,
And Broken Foot,
Weeps The Tree,
Of A Thousand Tears,
When Thorns For A King,
Twisted For A Crown,
Placed Is It For Me?
Oh King Of The Jews,
Hence Arms Out Stretched,
To The Waiting Watching,
That Will Surely Follow,
Bearing Their Wounds,
Of The Master,
When Love Is Purple,
This Good Friday,
Dear Virgin!

THE CROSS

```
        XXXXX
        XXXXX
        XXXXX
XXXXX           XXXXX
XXXXX           XXXXX
        XXXXX
        XXXXX
        XXXXX
        XXXXX
        XXXXX
```

A CURSE CONCEIVED

A Roman Cross,
Was A Curse Conceived,
Designed In Hell,
By Satan,
Constructed By Man,
Was The Derelict Tree,
For Christ Our Saviour,
To Hang,
For His World,
His World To Redeem,
With Arms Outstretched,
In Love Desiring,

    Most Unknown!

JESUS CHRIST

Jesus Christ,
Christmas Is,
The Shepherds hillside visitation,

Come now Emanuel,
And bring your Dazzling Light,

Baptizing,
Carpenter,
With such Flame,
Be the anointed Nazarene,
Kissed 'n' Stripped,
For your Tangled Crown,

I must now know,
Did you choose and make Salvations
                              Tree,

To Grow?
For if you did?
This is now such a Gospel

When Caravans and Kings,
Did Ride.

DERELICT MAN

Have you been to the Gibbet Tree,
And seen the Derelict Man taste his wine,
Crowned in thorns,
Busy, dying bruised and broken?

Derelict of Daddy,
Derelict of Man,

Is this really our holy Lamb of God,
Stepping into the rubbish that is now our lives?
You who celebrate you know not what,
If you have not already been to the Gibbet Tree,

Derelict of Daddy,
Derelict of Man,

Now the Gibbet Tree is empty,
Our God will come again, not riding on a pony,
But as Captain of his Daddy's Army.

WAR IS OVER

Red Are Those Poppies,
That Fell,
Fell,
On Flanders Fields,
For They Were Petals Of Blood,
Like Scarlet,
Now Our Great War Is Over,
On The Cold,
And Cruel Ground,

For I Can Hear The Birds,
In Their Hedgerows,
And Trees,
Hedgerows And Trees,
Singing Their Song,
Singing Their Song,
A New Song,

For Peace Has Come,
Come At Last,
At Last,
   Last!

PURPLE FRIDAY
(Poem For Good Friday)

Human Hands,
Just As Our Hands,
Were The Carpenters Hand,
Healing Hands,
Pierced Hands,
Is This Our Lords Hands,
Carrying The Marks Man!

THE CHAPEL IN THE ROCK

The Chapel in the
                Rock,

Hewn,

Is my Cavern in the
                Rock,

Burns Moses Flame,

No longer a Tomb,

Is my Bolder in the
                Rock,

Power in the
                Rock,

Over Easter Days,

Sung by Jesu's Song,

A glorious   Song,

Is my Cavern in the
                Rock,

This Symphony,

On Pebbles Cast,

Beaches when,

Tides are left,

Bottles Green,

Messages,

Is my Cavern in the
                        Rock,

The Chapel in the
                        Rock.

                                    Written at Lee Abbey Devon.

TOUCH STONE POEM

Pebble in a Pocket,
Clasp and hold,
Pain, 'tis etched all over you,
Left over of Sin,
Written on the Fore head,
Counted on hairs,
Seen in he Eye,
And broken of Body,
Smelling of Myrrh,
By way of the Christ Child,
Painting your Faces with words!!
With words,
Softly spoken,,
A Man acquainted with sorrow.

AND GOD CAME DOWN TO EARTH ONE DAY
(A Christmas Poem - The True Christmas)

And God Came Down To Earth One Day,
                         To Earth He Came,

For He Messed With The Bloody After Birth,
                                   All That Shit,

To Lie On One Little Ole Bed Of Straw,
For The Wise an' The Shepherds did Awe,

Behind Really The Most In Significant Inn,
Mixing With The Most In Significant Of People,

Labouring Hard At The Most In Significant Of Jobs,
In The Most Unholy Of Empires,

To Preach And Tell Of His Way,
Away We Did Not Know,

For Then We Stumbled In Darkness,
For Now We Walk In The Light Of His Star,

Knowing Our God Is Everywhere,
For He Created Us This Way,

To Work With Our Neighbour,
Where Gods Love A-Bounds.

A TAKE ON THE NATIVITY
(A Poem For The Christmas Season)

Huddled,
Refugees Gather,
For There Is A Mother,
A Virgin,
Get Your Head Around That?

For I Am Their Christmas Tree,
Bowed Low,
Heavy With Sin,
For They Shall Use Me,
To Crucify My Lord,
The Powers That Be,

And There Are Shepherds,
Ever So Humble,
Really Humble,
In Their Dirt,
Employed By The Temple,

And There Are Said To Be Kings,
Following A Mysterious Light,
Coming With Caravans Of Camels,

Though None Of This Makes Much Sense,
Just To Visit A Babe?
And A Baby Boy,
      At That,
For The Nutcracker is Dancing Still,   On,   And On!

HOLY SATURDAY

God Is Dead,
Completely Dead,
On Holy Saturday,

Pray,
Digest This,
If You May?

God Is Dead,
Completely Dead,
On Holy Saturday,

Pray,
Digest This,
If You May?

For He No Longer Hangs,
From The Old Gibbet Tree,

Pray,
Digest This,
If You May?

But Cradled In Mary His Mothers,
Becoming Veiled Tears To Be,

Pray,
Digest This,
If You May?

For Dark Was His Caver-ness Tomb To Lay,
When Preaching In Hells Deep Fire,
To Those Beloved Saints By Him,
That Had Fallen A Sleep,

Pray,
Digest This,
If You May?

For Our God That Was Dead,
Completely Dead,
Shall Rise From The Ground,
Though The Earth Be Cold,

Pray,
Digest This,
If You May?

He Shall Rise,
Bringing Warmth And New Light,
To His Garden,
Will The Gardener,

Pray,
Digest This,
If You May?

RISEN
(A Poem For Easter Day)

And His Tomb Was Empty!!

HAVE YOU SEEN THE LION?

Have you seen the Lion,
With your own Eyes?

A SEASON OF OPTIMISM AND JOY

Bird Song Sweet,
Fags Papers 'n' Litter,
Scat,
And Run,
Like The Dogs,
Over The Turf,
The Green, Green Turf,
Wild Like The Wind,
To The Earth,
When Soaking The Shower,
Rooting 'n' Shooting,
New Life,
As The Kids
In This Season,
A Season Of Optimism,
      And Joy,

For The Ground Is A Warming,
Warming,
The Trees Are In Bud,
Bloomin'
Reaching Up,
Tall,

To Face That Bright Orange Ball,
Like All Manner Of Drops,
So White,
Snow White,
Virgin White,

Trumpeting,
Trumpeting In,
With Its Fan Fare,
So Proud,
So Loud,
Lightening Days Have Arrived,
With Spring In The Gardens,
                    And Park!

                              Barnstaple
                              Rock Park
                            In Spring Time

FOUR LETTERS

FoUr LeTtErS.

F
o
U
r

L
e
T
t
E
r

SaYs Love!

THE SUN

My Friend The Sun,
Is Glorious And Round,
And Strong,
When Shadows Are Long,
And Canopy's Oh So Green,
And All Is Blooming Lovely,
Oh Smell The Roses Dearest,
For Then We'll Eat Nothing But Ice Cream,
In These Our Halycon Days Of Summer,
When All Seems Well With The World.

BOSCASTLE

Boscastle,

Witches,

And Flood,

Cornish,

And Fishers,

Tourists,

And Smugglers,

Star Gaze-y Pie,

And Pasties,

The Black Headed Circle,

On This Cove,

Upon Cove!

WORTH

Uniform,

IS,

WoRtH,

mOrE,

THAN,

a,

MAN !!!

MARIUPOL

And The Poet Survives,
By The Blood Of His Song,
In The Rains That Are The Rivers,
                That Fall,

Hunting For Bread,
In The Wintered Springs,
That The Aliens Bring,

For What Cannot Be Let Go!
Must Be Waved On The Train,

Besieging,

What Is Dust 'n' Capital Rubble,
That Is,
      Old Mariupol!

Putin's War
With Ukraine
22

BUTTER FLY BOMBS

Ukraine,

    I Have No House,
    No Home,
    To Call My Own,
    No Car,
    No Foot,
    Mr. Putin,

And I Have Been Taught,
That Butter Fly Bombs,
    Have Been Band!

RUSSIA THE GREAT BEAR

Oh My Dear,
It's Russia The Great Bear,
          With Raids,

Missile Strikes,
And War,
Has Come,
To This Orthodox Land,
See From Your Window,
          And Pray,

That The Clowns Shall Go Away,
For What Cannot Be Let Go,
Must Be Let Go,

In War,
Ruin And Rubble,
Of Ukraine,
Twenty Two,
Twenty Two,
          Friend,

Oh How We Weep,
          For You!

THE NAKED LADY

The Naked Lady,
A Bronze,
She Sat On The Stairs,
Half Way Up The Stairs,
Did Our Naked Lady,
And Looked so Bear,

For She Sat On The Mule Post,
Half Way Up,
Or Was It Down The Stairs,
She Looked So Gracious,
Was Our Naked Lady,
And I'm almost Certain,
She's Winked At Me,
A That Time or Two!

TO PRAY AS YOU GO

Oh Busy London Town,
Says,
Pray As You Go,
Have You Ever Walked In Off The Side Walk?
To Pray As You Go,
Stepping Over The Night Sleepers?
Beggars?
And Buskers?
To Pray As You Go,
Clasping Your Hands In Prayer,
To Kneel,
To Sit,
And To Stand,
There,
In Prayer,
For Sake Of Your Spirit,
For Sake Of Your Soul,
However You May Persevere Your God?
For There You Are In The House Of The Lord,
A While,
Tell Me,
Where Are You?
St. Brides,
A while,
Or Is It Another Great London Church?
                    On The App!

        The London Map App Of Churches

TURNING THE TIDE
(Into Tomorrow
A Chapter Of Possibilities
Twenty First Century)

Oh Where Is Our Shoreline?
As We Are On The Hedge,
Of A Brave New World,
Of Discovery's,
In spite Of Famine,
        And War,

We Now Come Up With New MEds,
Pushing Back The Realms Of Science,
And Technology,
As Man Becomes His Own Sweet God,

Exploding,
Surfing,
Stepping Back Into Space,
To The Moon,
And Beyond,

Just As Gaia,
Reappears,
On Placard And Bill Board,
              Greening,

And Still We Dance,
Carolling,
Carolling,

On,
On,
Into Our Brave New World,
Of Tomorrows Possibilities!

ADMIRAL

Coloured Fly,
Winged Admiral,
Oh Leave,
Pray Take Our Summer,
           South,

And Bring Your Swift Return!

OH POOR VENICE

Oh Poor Venice,
Sweet Venice,
You Are But Trampled Under Foot,
Flooded With Tourists,
Of Foot,
With Your Gondola's Of Water,
And Rippling Veins of Canals,
When Taken From Bridges,
Is Your Wonderful Bridge Of Sizes,
Having Coffee In St. Marks Square,
Whilst The Bell Dongs For The People,
All Of Thong,
Was This A Postcard Scene,
Of Just Ice cream,
Of Lovers In Bliss,
Beneath The Doges Palace,
The Adriatic Sun Lowers,
Pink In All Her Glory,
With A Cruise Ship Of Haze,
In Our Distance,
Ancient Homes Are Weeping,
Of Their Tourists Now,
           Now,

To Be Shot Of Them,
Knowing One Can't Do Without Them,
Sinking,
Oh Sinking Beneath Their Prints,
Oh Poor Venice,

Sweet Venice,
You Are But Trampled Under Foot.

THE OLD GREY POT

I am On The Shelf,
Nothing But A Pot,
Somewhat Cracked,
And Chipped,
Forgotten,
My Colour Grey Like Slip,
Waiting,
Waiting,
To Be Thrown Away,
         Away,

Like Yesterday,
A Pot With No Colour,
No Future,
No Life,
Although I Was Spun Into Life,
By A Potter,

An Artisan One Might Say,
From Clay,
With His Clay,
Clay In His Hands,
So Nimble,
Moulding,
Then Fired And Baked Into Life,

But Oh Now Alas,
I am On The Shelf,
Not Used,

But Waiting,
Waiting,
To Be Thrown Away,
          Away,

Somewhat Like Yesterday,
Yesterday,
It Can Only Be A Mete-Far,
But Never Told,
Or Spoken Of,
Is This My Story Uttered In
                    Jest!

THE GIRL

The Girl Came Out Of The Dream,
                            To Bloom,

As The Woman,
        Walking!

THE MISSING PIECE

Was The Missing Piece,
Dear To Me,
Was The Missing Piece,
When Gone,
Large To Me,
That Hole,
Was She,
When Gone,

For Then Grief,
Crept In,
Ugly And Blank,
Was The Void,
For The Large Was That Space,
Now Heard-er To Fill,
The Missing Piece!

        Mother's Dementia

UNIFORM

You who wear uniform
You have no choice,
For you have already made your choice.
To put on your uniform,
And make known your colour shown.
You who wear uniform
You have no view,
When you put on your uniform.
For your view has then become
Our State's view,
And made opinion known its colour shown.
You who wear uniform
You dance on strings,
You poor little things.
Then beg to play,
Killing, cloth rather than creed
And makin' known whose colour shown.

WHO?
(The Great War, 1914-18)

Who?
    Dies On The Wire,
    The Horrible Wire,
    Tangled in Blood,
    They Lay,
    Two A-Penny,
    The Red Poppies,
    That Fall,
    Like The Rains,
    In No Man's Land,
    On Lads As Young As I,

Who?
    Dies On The Wire!

ACTOR

Where Is Thy True Face?
Behind The Mask,
Entering In,
Stage Right,
Or Left,
You Goon,
Of A Clown,

Hide Your Feelings,
Hide Your Face!

FLOYD

Floyd,

Floyd,

He Cried,

Sayin',

"I can't Breathe",

"I can't Breathe",

Then he Died,

Died,

In Custody,

In Custody,

He Died,

To Protests and Fire,

Fire,

He Died,

And the Nations Cried!

Cried!

For Floyd,

George Floyd,

With Anger and Pain,

Anger and Pain,

Sayin',

"BlAcK LiVeS MaTtEr",

"MaTtEr",

"MaTtEr"!!!

THE REFUGEE

I am a Refugee,
A drop in a Human Sea,
Lost in the Crowd,
Of Cameras 'n' faces,
Media speak,

'Quickly'

With nothing,
Did,
We come,
Just a drop in a Human Sea,
My Parents and me,
A Carpenters Son,
'Running,'
From a murderous King,

To tear gas 'n' wire.
They didn't want us there
One more drop in a Human Sea,
And so to Egypt's shores
                'We came,'

Wintering there,
For three long years,
Did the drop in a Human Sea,
Till I was grown,
            My name,
                  'Jesus'.

NEVER

"NeVer Be A By StAndER"

MIGRANTS
(Peoples 'n' Their Little Boats)

Oh White Cliffs,
Dinghy, Vessels By The Ord,
Beckon 'n' Shine,
Attempting The Murderous Root,
To Live, To Shine,

Again Over Our Seas,
To Shine,
Amid a People Most Strange,
A Clouded Land - To Settle,
The Migrants Flee,
Oh Paying Their Godless Root
                        To Flee!

AFRICAN MAN

Wide is My Nose,
And Tight is My Hair,
Now Large is My Print,
As I stand so tall,
For I want to rectify My Sociology,
Then I want to rectify My Philosophy,
For I am proud,
I am twenty first Centre Man,
No longer Gods Ape Man,
For I want to play My Part,
With Tattoo, Pipe, 'n' Liquor,
I want to benefit Society,
I am your Brother,
No longer a Slave,
But a Free Man,
                Walkin',
                          Walkin'.

Out from the Plain,
The Plains of Africa!

PUBLIC LIMITED COMPANY

The UK P. L. C.
Is Like A Many Layered Onion,

Therefore Friend,

Don't Be COLOUR BLIND!

HANDS OF TIME
(Having Just One Candle, To The Clown)

It Is A Miracle To Be Alive,
For Our Life Is So Short,
Then Be Astonished Friend,
And Live It,
Live It,
Whilst One May,
For Your Love Hearts Are Marked,
Scribed To The Tree,
Whilst Musing Over The Five Bar Gate,
To Those Whom Tolled,
The Dead Man's Story,
For They Were Awful Sorrow,
For He Had Been Dead From The Neck
                          Up,

This Dancing,
Dancing Man,
Having Just One Candle,
      To The Clown!!

        Dedicated To Our Man Of Butterfly Mind

OH MOTHER OF MINE
(Dementia)

Oh When All At Once,
I Looked Into That Mirror,
Of Mine,
And Saw Those Dark Eyes,
those Deep Dark Set Eyes,
Staring Back,
Back At Me,
With Your Wretched Frown,
Of Puzzlement,
And It Pains Me,
        So,

Mother,
Oh Mother Of Mine,
Lost,
Beyond,
In Your Tragic Condition,
Of A Timeless World Of Mist,
        And Song,

For It Is As If The Lights Are On,
Although There's No One In?
Mother,
Oh Mother Of Mine,
For I am Your Son,
Your First Born Son!

THE COLOURS

Cool,
Grey,
Soldiering,
Are The Coats,
Of The Colours,

Is Our Day,
Of November,
Honouring The Fallen,
For The Air Is Still,
          Calm,

As The Coloured Leaves
                Blow,

Is This The Calm,
Before the Winter?

                              Remembrance Day
                                        2022

WORDS, THE BLOOD THAT RUNS THROUGH MY VEINS

Oh I Don't Get Out That Much,
I Don't Have Much Choice You See,
A Slave To This I am,
For I am Compelled To Sit,
And Have A Cigar To Many,

Oh Dear Reader Of Mine!!

FLOTSAM 'N' JETSAM.

Sea blown, wind blown,
God what have we done?
Plastic 'n' cans
Bits of nets and broken bottles
Jagged to the edge,
Makes you think,
God what have we done?

Look at the litter strewn,
Birds oiled in decay,
Flotsam 'n' Jetsam
Fancy names for our fancy rubbish.

Huge trees somehow coughed up and regurgitating
Spilling out of the tide
Like an elephant's skull, from an elephant's graveyard,
Gnarled to the tough, telling a different story.

Sea blown, wind blown
God what have we done?
Plastic 'n' cans
They scatter and they run across the sands,
Flotsam 'n' Jetsam
Fancy names for our Fancy Rubbish.

God said it was good,
God what have we done?

WATER

Droplet,
See It Spout,
Cooling,
Lapping,
Tumbling,
Flooding,
Water, Water,
Everywhere,
Flowing Down,
Now Part Of My River,
Under Those Arches,
To The Salt Sea Air,
With Your Otters,
    Mr. Brown,

In Rings Of Bright Waters,
Springing Up,
Lashing Down,
Is Are Those Rains,
Under Those Arches,
Now Part Of My River,
Oh Tarrant Of Rain,
Past My Chimney,
And Town,
With Your Otters,
Oh Crossing Those Wretched Sandbanks,
                  Mr. Brown!

CONSTANT

ThE wInd Is A CONSTANT!
                        B
                        R
                        e
                         E
                          e
                           z
                           e.

AUTUMNAL WOODLAND

When The Cool Breezes Blow,
Autumn Shows You Are,
In Colour Come,
Moist And Rest,
Showing now,
Fragrant Woodland Of Fungi,
Slow,
Spout Upon The Green Man's Tree,

And Now Those Animals Shall Sleep.
Just That Little Bit Longer,
And Those Rivers Shall Flow,
And Chuckle like drains,
Just A Little Bit Faster,

For 'tis Because Our Year,
She Is Just That Bit Older,
Amid Crimson Reds,
And Golden Browns,
Of Nuts And Conkers,
There To Lay,
On Gods Good Earth,

 Pray,
Smell,
To Learn,
Listen,
To Watch,
The Birds Are Quartering,

Sauntering,
Preparing,
With Other Creatures,
Of The Woodland,
For Winters,
Ices Return,

For there's More To Meet This Season,
Than What Meets Ones Eye?
Dear Friends,
Of Toffee Apples-Bobing,
To Folklore,
Sith Sawyers 'n' Tales,
Are You Covens,
Gathering,
Around The Ole Camp Fire!

THE BEGINNING OF US!

We Are All In Our Great Grandmothers
                               Womb,

Just Take A Little Time Out,
To Think About It!

THOSE FAMILY CHRISTMASES

Oh Where Have They Gone,
Those Family Christmases,
     Of Now Long Ago?

Of Tinsel And Glitter.
Of Bond Cars,
And China Dolls,
And Engines Too,

Oh Where Have They Gone,
Those Family Christmases,
     Of Now Long Ago?

Of Wishbone Dinners,
And Party Hats,
And Rather Silly Games,
Beneath The Mistletoe And Wine,

Oh Where Have They Gone,
Those Family Christmases,
     Of Now Long Ago?

When Wrapped Around It,
Was A Decorated Tree,
From Which Your Family Hung,
Whilst Playing The Old Joanna
              There!

Xmas
22

LOUISE
(A Poem of Day Dreams)

I walked with Louise, and We sang until Morning,
Songs of the river, and songs of the night,
Over golden trod meadows,
In promise of colour,
Where Moon is a-eclipsing dew drops of grasses,

Reflecting the Faces She has a-spoken,
In myriad of Stars,
A Million and one,
For Velvet the night,
A pattern of day,

So We sang until Morning,
Songs of the night,
And dreamed of sleep,
And Orbits to come, To come,

For then The Hills Would Be Alive,
To The Sound Of Music,
Playing, Playing,
Softly,
In Our Fragile Memories,
Was that Old Piano!
        Piano!
That dear Niece of Mine!!

                        Miss. Katie Louise Fry
                      On The Eve Of Her Wedding

NATHAN THE NOISE

Nathan The Noise,
Was A Sweet Young Boys,
With Bright Blue Eyes,
And Ginger Hairs,
Who Went And Travelled A-Far,
With Bex The X,
Sealed With A Loving Kiss,
Ending Up As They Did,
High On A Wall,
The Great Wall Of Old China Town,
Seen From Space,
God What A Race,

And I Have No Doubt,
That Our Nathan Noise,
Could Travel Into Space,
That He Surely Would,
If He Only Could?

Our Nephew

TWINS

What Is It like My Friends,
To Have Another Face Like Yours?
Walking,
Sleeping,
Spinning,
Revolving In Oribit,
In Tme And Space,
Upon This Oh So Bizzar Planet Of Ours,
When Your Not Really Alike,
                Are You?

Yes Your Parents May Have Dressed You?
And Combed Your Hair,
Those Golden Hairs,
That Shine So Bright,
For Those Gorges Photo's,
Sent To Granny At Christmas,
But Then You Are Not Really A like,
                Are You?

For Me And Oreo We've Watched You Grow,
Up,
Up,
Up,
And Away,
Wearing Different Garments And Clothes,

My Friends,
With Your Different Jobs,

Hobbies And Interests,
For You Have Grown To Be,
So Nice Young Men!

                    Our Nephews In London Town

SADNESS IN THE MARGINS

Sadness In The Margins,
Speaks Of Loss,
And Cemetery Fields,
Lofty Over Me,
Hang Like A Cloud,
An Old Grey Cloud,
For We No Longer See Him,
Packing About The Streets,
The Desolate Streets,
With His Friendly Face,
          That Is,

Sadness In The Margins.

                        Remembering Uncle

OH THE KIDS TO DAY

Oh The Kids To Day,
Look Feed Up,
Oh The Kids To Day,
Look Cheesed Off,
With Faces As Long As Fiddles,
For Where Has The Smile Of Youth Been Taken?
For Now They Just Seem,
Dead From The Neck Up,
For Nor Do They Play Hop Scotch In The Yard,
What A Miserable Lot They Seem,

For In My Day,
We Had The Cane,
As Well As Jammy And Ridd To Box Our Ears,
And Then You Could Still Get Dunk Down,
The Nearest Dirty Lav,
Head First,
Like Ole Vinsen,
On That Tuesday Afternoon,

No Kids To Day,
Don't Know They're Born To Day,
For All They Are,
Is Tested,
And Tested,
All Day,

Oh The Kids To Day,
Know Nothing About Mitching Off German,

Only Then to Hide Down The Library,
To Watch The Lasses At Gym,
In Those Large Navy Knicks,
Whilst You Would Then Go And Steel A Fag And A Kiss,
From Pauline Behind The Drama Hall,

Being Tested,
And Tested,
From Morn To Night,
What Does That Prove?

I'll Tell You,
Then If You Don't Already Know,
With Each Test One Takes,
One Should Get Better,
And As For Exams,
And Letters After Ones Name,
They're Just Pieces Of Paper,
And So Its All Bull Shit To Me,

For The Kids To Day,
Don't Seem To Know Anything,
After All History Started With Them,
Nor Do They Look As If They Trust Anyone,
            What A God Damn Shame,

None Of Them Have Kicked A Ball In The Back Alley,
Or Run Wild Threw The Country Meadows And Fields,
Catching Salmon For Their Tea,

After All Mummy And Daddy Are Scared To Let Them Out,
It's As I Say,
Its All Bull Shit To Me,

For It Isn't Where You Start,
But Where You Finish,
And As I Gaze Around Me To Day,
Some Of The Kids From My Class,
Left Without A Bean In Their Pocket,
And They May Still Not Be Able To Read Or Write To Day,
Yet They Hold Down Jobs,
Run Business,
Or Even Run Their Own Companies,
Ducking And Diving As They Do,
On The Street Corner,
Making Lots Of Filthy Lucher!!

THE OLD CROW

Black,
Black,
Was The Old Crow,
That Pecked,
And Pecked At The Turf,
Hard Winters Turf,
Which Gave No Ground,
So He Danced,
And Danced,
The Hour Long,
Pecking,
Pecking,
For Worms,
And Grubs to Feed,
Hopping,
Hopping,
Mad Was He,
When I Did Spy Him Last,
In That Chill,
Chill Morn!

IN THE ARRIVAL

Winter Has Come,
The Leaves Are Scat,
The Trees Are Naked,
As The Charcoal Morning,
In The Stillness Of The Air,
Kind Of Quiet,
When All Was Spoken,
For Ones Self,
In The Arrival,

And The Passers By,
Seemed Largely Wrapped Up
                          Well,

In This Early December Day,
Just As The Jackdaw,
The Crow,
And The Raven,
The Birds Of Darkness,
Death,
And Winter,
Sauntered,
Sauntered,
Quartering,
Quartering,
About Us,
With Their Usual Hop Skip,
                  And A Jump,

Whilst A Lone Mercurial Magpie Swooped In,
On A Top Most Branch,
And With That I Did Notice Him,
For Then My Mood Turned,
Again Most Sombre,
For What Sorrow Would He Bring?

OXFORD

Isis,

        Mirage Floating,

                Bathed In All Its Glory,

Dreaming Spires,

        Come Seats Of Precious Learning.

67

Hippies Walked,
That Golden Mile,
Of Sunset and Dune,
Smoking Dope,
To the Youth Hostel,
And Ripple,
Wearin' Flowers in their hair,
For The Times were a-Changing,
Utterin' Love and Peace,
                'Man,'

In that year of 67,
        67!

                              Childhood Memory
                                          Instow

A MOST PASSIVE LOT

Having a Fag,
In the Park,
Just Lovely,
Seeing The Dogs,
   Run,

And Bound,
After Balls,
Watching Them Shit,
Among Childhood Play.
Seeing Them Mate,
Their Owners Are a Most Passive,
        Lot,

Whilst The Leaves Turn,
Crimson,
Golden Brown,
Wistful,
In There Lot,
Beneath Clouded Skies

Telling Their Story,
Of Man,
And His Humanity To Man,
Up along,
Down Along,
Rivers And Moors,
Where Trees Were Once,
There is Nothing But Factories,

    And Chimney Towers,

For Once God Said,
It Was Good,
God What Have We Now?
Now The Bleeding Earth Is On Fire,
And The Ice,
Is Melting,
Melting!

                                  For COP-22

TAW VALE, AND RETURN

Winsome,

Along Taw Vale,
In Seasons Under The Sun,
Beside The River,
And In Coming Tide,
With Its Breeze,
        Breeze,

In Coming Breeze,
Then To Cross The Square,
                There,

Beneath Old Father Time,
Deceiving The Time,
Ole Master Of Time,

Only To Reach The Lights,
The Flickering,
Flickering,
Red,
Yellow,
And Green Lights,
Oh How Obscene,

I've Reached The Busy Town,
Cross Street,
High Street,
And The Street of Nineteenth Century Joy,

Oh How Obscene,
To Reach The Street Of Nineteenth Century Joy,

The To Return The Same Way,
Laden,
Journey Back Through The Park,
                  Is My Way,

Running Back Along The Old Tarmac Path,
Past The Barking,
Barking Yelping Dogs,
Curiosity Dogs,
Dogs Of Our Day,
What A Tremendous Day!

HAVE YOU

Oh Have You Seen The Girls That Cried?

WOMEN

Women,
        Function As A Looking Glass!

SHADOW FLY
(Red Admiral)

Gentile,
Shadow Fly,
Crimson Red,
This Butter Fly,
Flies,
In Front Of The Golden Ball,
          Of Summer,

Gentile,
Shadow Fly,
Crimson Red.
Scorched Its Wings,
To Fly,
But Always Less Than Its
          Shadow,

Winged,
Summer Fly!

RED SENTINEL

Bells,
Thatch,
Crown and Sceptre
Idle,
Pony's,
Drink,
Where the Mirror Shines
Over Stag Dew Falls,
          Red,

Then Travel High,
And Travel Long,
Through Hamlet small,
And Barrows Long,
Loosing Days,
Over Weir,
By way of the Stones,

Where the Mirror Shines,
Spilt of Blood,
Through haze of misty blue,
Telling our Story,
Our ancient Story,
In a fragrance only for you,
In Purple and Blue,

Leaving Echoing Stones,
To Cast their Hunted Shadow
Ruins, though True,

For those who walk,
In tempered steps,
Alone with you..

The Red Deer
An Exmoor Stag

SOMERS FALL

Autumn day, harvest, Autumn gold,
Taste,
Furnished burnished beech bronze,
Tinted in the shadow lands,
Mellow mists low where pleasant waters flow.

Reminiscences, toast of a Puritan past,
In hostelries now, built as stations then.
Colour my memory with your New Model Army.
A fragment lost like Somers Past.

Journey on to Dulverton, and the sound of the distant rut
Where the old clapper Bridge still stands to serve and to span,
                              The Barle,
Trippers now.

Though at the Trigg spot, he light fades,
Way like my view, like my words running,
Like the river runs to the Sea, to the Sea.

                            First Poem Published
                Written At The White Horse Exford

78 DAYS
(Or Instant Trinity)

Beech Leaves,
And Trees,
Coloured Falling Leaves,
What Comes Around,
Goes Around,

Or Instant Trinity,
Born Unto Your Finger Tips,
Stirred In Your Cup,
Makes Body The Bread,
Broken At The Alter,
    'Father'

Seventy Eight Days,
To Christmas,
Like Scaring Nine Year Olds,
   At Our Door!

        To Christmas Day

OLD PEAT

Darken Organic,
Soil Of My Blood,
Grow Moist Mysterious Moor,
Crumble Rich,
Between Finger 'n' Thumb,
                      Dug,

To Feed My Clay,
Oh Soil Of My Blood,
Burning In Winters Chill,
For It's Then,
With Tears,
We Embrace!

SKETCHING OLE STICK JAW
(Syd Trewin Of Lydford Town-Dartmoor)

Granite,
Dartmoor Ran Through His Vines,
Like Its Peat That He Had Once Burnt
                In A Season,

For He Loved His Castle,
His Jar,
And His Whiskey,
Did Timeless Ole Stick Jaw,
Walking With Wide Gate That Crooked Mile,
As He Smoked His Beloved Pipe,
Looking Somewhat Like Pop Pie,
Beneath His Cap,
With Worn And Weather Wind Chiselled Face,

He Didn't Care Much For The Sheep,
Nor For The Ponies That Roamed,
To The Sounds Of The Streams,
Giggling With Laughter,
At The New Day,

No Ole Stick Jaw As We Called Him,
In Those Now Far Off Days,
Cared For His Walls,
Those Dry Stone Walls,
Of The Moor,
Did Our Gruff Ole Syd Trewin,

Dividing Sheep From Tor,
Carpeted In Purple,
As He Made and Mended His Walls,
Those Dry Stone Walls,
Of The Moor,

For The Moor Was Timeless Of Man,
Prehistoric To Its Self,
Lonely And For Bolding,
And Told Its Tales Of Folk Law,
When The Devil Went Riding Through Here,
Together With Those Walls,
 Tumbling Grey Walls,

Yes, Ole Stick Jaw,
Made And Mended Those Walls,
Those Dry Stones Walls,
Of The Moor,
Labouring Hard,
As He Did For Others,
Those Who Would Surely Come,
After He,

As He Had Come,
Taking His Place,
In Moorland Order,
Like Stones In The Wall,
            Timeless,

Prehistoric,
Were Their Mood So Grey,

Like Stick Ole Jaw,
Ashen With Backie,
And With Age,
As He Listened,
Taking Breath To Catch The Song Of
 Of The Moor,
The High Moor,

Knowing Men's Days Are But Short,
He Could Hear The Muffled Bells In Village,
Beneath The Rolling Dartmoor Mists That Hung,

For One More Friend Lay Quietly Sleeping,
                              Sleeping!

ALONG THE GRANITE WAY
(A Lydford Rabble)

To Set The Scene,
Caught Up Was I,
In My Muse,
I Scrabbled Up There,
Alongside Widgery,
And His Golden Cross Of Jubilee,

 Once There,
I Could Be Free,
With Blessing My Friend,
With Black Faced,
And Those Five Pointers,
On A Carpet Of Purple,

Walking 'n' Wandering,
As I Did,
Between The Tors,
And Moors,
Of Granite Walls,
Through The Woodland,
        Of Fungi,

And Moss,
For There again,
The Air Was Clear,
Rooted In My Birth,
At The Granite Way,
For There Indeed My Journey's

Had Begun,

When Listening To Those Curlews Call,
Or The Buzzards Circle,
Over Head Stone Wall,
Beside My Ribbons Of Stream,
    A-Flow,

High With a-Wash,
Autumns Wash,
Of Leaves,
Coloured Leaves,
Is The Pallet Now,
Through This Rollin' Mist,
   Painted Now,

At This Time Of Year,
For There Was My Journey's Way,
Rooted Of My Birth,
Both In The Language I Heard,
And The Song That Was Sung,
For There Was a Community Here,
People You Would Find,
Along Lives Road,
And Even Those Queer Ghosts,
You Would Have Liked To Have Known,
Along Lives Journey's Way,

Either In Their Homes,
At St. Michael Dela-Rupe,
Watchin' On

Or Even Down At The Castle,
 The Nicholls,
Or Even At The Old Mucky Duck,
Sharin' The Laughter 'n' Tears,
And Raisin' Just Well Lets Say,
         One Jar To Many,

For There,
At The Old Mucky Duck,
The Lines Would Cross,
Crossing My Palm With Silver,
And Say, A-Long Farewell,
To Archimedes And His Pump,
Along The Granite Way!!

                      Lydford, Devon
                Part Of The Granite Way

ARCHIMEDES PUMP

Reds, Brown,
Greens 'n' Gold,
Leaves,
Do they dance?
Do they Fall?
Autumn,
Blown,
Wisp full Ridge
Of Showers Spills,
Splash,
On this my Granite Ways,
Down Around Mill,
Beside our gurgling Lyd,
Your Waters hang,
Archimedes Pump.

                                        Lydford Mill

THE TALE OF POOR WILFRED
(Just A Country Boy Was He)

Oh I Have A Tale Of Woe To Tell,
Just Of A Country Boy Was He,
    His Name,

Oh Poor Wilfred Was His Name,
And Not So Very Long Ago,
A Thatchers Son Was He,
Growing Beside The Stream 'n' Rivers
      There,

He Played And Played,
That Son Of Dear Ole Darty Moor,
At The Town,
He Called Lydford Town,
For I like To Think That He Was Somewhat Innocent,
Was Oh Poor Wilfred Of The Moor,

Writing His Poetry 'n' Song,
To Share,
In Hostelries Of His Day,
    There,

For Cutting His Reed,
And Taking His Cider,
For The Reed And The Song,
Flowed Through The Veins Of The Moor,

Oh And Then One Fateful August Day Happened,

When The Moorland Carpet Was Purple,
Ole Poor Wilfred Marched Off To War,
Leaving That Which He Knew,
    Far Behind Him There,

In The War They Said, "Would Be Over In Time For Christmas",
Dear Wilfred Was To Fight With The Hun,
In That Same War That Would End All Wars,
His Head Went Over The Top,
Climbing The Wire,
And Screaming,
Wilfred Ran The Enemy Through,
With That His Binet Of Steel,
Seeing Those Mates He Knew Die,
From Those Brave Royal Warwickshire's,
For The Enemies Machine Guns Did Spit,
Poppies Of Blood,
As The Fallen,

For A Far From Homes He Knew,
He Was,
When Letters And Parcel's From Did Come,
Whilst Wearing That Uniform Of His King,
                      So Proud,

And So He Wrote Home To Mum One Day,
Telling Her And Dad One Day,
That War Would Soon Be Over,
Yes Soon He Enough,
And Not To Worry,

There,

But Then Alas Poor Dear Wilfred,
Spluttered,
And Sneezed,
And Sneezed,
And Coughed All Day,
To He Died All Day,
All Day,
At Lark Hill Hospital,

Leaving His Poor Father Frank,
To Listen To The Larks Ascending,
Ascending There,
Over Good Old Darty Moor!

Frank Wilfred Fry
Born 1899
Died Nov 1918

AT THE CHURCH OF MY FORE FATHERS
(St. Petroc's Lydford, Devon)

As I Strolled Past The Twelve Yew,
Counted Now For The Apostles,
The Watchmaker Was Sleeping Peaceful In His Tomb,

And So I Entered The Church Of My Fore Fathers,
For There I Did Glance Up At The Dark Wooden Screen,
And The Stained Glass Window Of The Sower And His Seed,

Beyond,

Telling The Story,
What A Parable,
I Thought,

For Walking Around This The Church Of St. Petroc's,
For Coming To Rest On The Font,
It Was Then I Pondered A Moment On All Its Baptisms,
Including My Own Father,
Edmund David,

He Had Been Born In The Year Of Three Kings,
Nestled In This Village Of Lydford,
Often Cloaked In The Mist Of The Moor,
For It Was This Church That Was The Cornerstone
                              Of This Small Community,

As For My Father He Had Gone On To Be A Soldier,
A Serving Police Officer,
To Have Been Married To Joy Elaine For Well Over
Sixty Years,
And They Themselves Had Three Sons,
Five Grand Children,
And One Great Grand Child,
And All This I Thought,
Came Out Of These Dark Morose Moors,
Where The Waters Are Clear,
For Life Can Be Hard In Winter,
And In Its Season The Carpets Are A Purple
                                        Haze!

GREYSTONE MEMORIES

A Dartmoor walk,
Goes a-wanderin',
To Greystone,
Hearing Echo's,
Through its Walls,
Of People's past,
Caught in the Snows,
Of Petroc's Bells,

Stepping out a Jar to many,
There the Lost Cord,
Was heard,
At Castles Keep,
A-Hunting, We did go,
Yonder Widgery,
At Lydford Town,
Where the blizzard wind,
Does rise 'n' howl,
Oh hanging Judge,
Forgetting not,
          "Dear Lionel"

Shepherd of your Sheep,
For a Dartmoor walk,
Goes a-wanderin'
Amid the purple heather,
Then takes my seat,
With a Cockade in my heart,
Of sweet Reminiscences,

For kissing Mary Jane neath the Mistletoe!!
          Caroling on, first Footing,
Into that New year.

                        Appears In Hidden Paths

SPIRITS HAVING FLOWN

It Happened On a Tuesday,
                Then,

When Me And My Brother,
Took a Journey,
        Then,

To Where Our Lyd Would Flow,
Rapid 'n' Deep,
Knowing Something Was Good,
                    There,

Although When We Arrived,
Did Not a Soul Exist,
But Echoing Walls,
And Boyhood Haunts,
        Of Old,

                Were Greystones,
                    Granite,

Just As The Will Of The Wisp,
Like Though Spirits That Had Flown,
Laughin' And Chucklin',
Those Ribbons Of Waters,
That Sang On Those Moor,
      With Heavens Gaze,

That Had Conceived Them So,

Long Since-In Days Ago,

And So We Raised Our Glasses,
Not Once But Twice,
        To Many,
There,

At Castles Keep,
To Bygone Spirits,
Having Flown,

Although Before We Turned,
To Say,
    'Farewell'

We Visited The Path,
      Of The Yew,

To Read The Names,
Of Those We Knew,
Etched In Colourless Grey,
Like The Moor
That Had Conceived Them So,

And So If We Were To Return,
That Same Way?
Only Those Spirits Would Know,
For The Journey was Long,
And Tiresome,
     Then,

And Alas Dear Brother,
I Soon Came To The Conclusion That Their Chapter
Had Ended,
And Therefore We Do Not Belong Here Any more,
For Those Spirits In Which We Had Known,
         Had Flown!

          Platinum Jubilee Week

THE WEALTH OF A DARTMOOR VILLAGE

I went for a walk alone, by myself,
Off the beaten track, where Roman feet once Trod,
Shrouded in the mists of time,

'Twas down yonder I wondered, under the old Southern
                                                Line Bride,

All that carries now is the haunting sound in folks'
                                        Memories,

When the sound of Steam was heard in this
Community,
When not one line did they have, but Two, Great
Western,
                                        And
Southern,

Summer was far gone, I soon came to the conclusion
                        That the Miller had gone
too,

Taken leave of his decaying Mill,
Beside The Lyd,

Over the water by way of an old wood bridge, I went on
my way,
Frightened by the sounds of my own two feet,
Crushen the fallen Autumn
Leaves,

And so I ran, breathless into light,
To a fork in the road,
Reminding me of chances taken and missed,

The Stately home of Squire Radford I passed,
"Ingo Brake" by name,

Into my head came many thoughts,
At the bottom of Gorge Hill, I paused,
To stop, to stare, into the rushing Gorge, where "The White Lady Falls"
    And "Devils Cauldron" swirls 'n' foams,

Up the other side I huffed and puffed
Again heading toward the Village from whence I came,
In times of Ethelred Coins were minted here,
St. Petroc's Church too, has many, many treasures,
Epitaph to of a watch makers Tomb, The Smithy's Wheel wright Stone!
Edmund Fry, lays here, Thatcher, and Folk Sing Supreme!
It was he who first came east across the Tamer, To view The Wealth of a Dartmoor Village.

Lydford, - England's largest Parish,
That covers most of the Duchy and its moods,
A Prison was Established here, for England's enemies, and her Outcasts,

Again I paused to stop 'n' to stare,

And look, at the Castle, Tasting Bitters,
For Judge Jefferys did hold his bloody assizes,
Casting People into dungeons deep, or to the
Hangman's Gallows,

As I wandered back through the Village, friends and
acquaintances I meet,
I stop and pass the time of day,
Exchanging news and gossip of the day,
When all at once, I muse again, concerning the
                                                     Tors

Arms and Doe, White and Brea,
Or Widgery if that is what you prefer,
Looking down on tumbled brook, and Granite Way,
                                       With her Cross,

Golden reign,

Beyond the Village, is the road, where coaches of old
once rolled,
                                    In search of Tin, Silver,
and Ore,

All that and very much more,
Is our Wealth, The Wealth of a Dartmoor Village.

                                                 Lydford 1981

THE MAGIC OF A DARTMOOR SCENE

You can see,
I can feel it,
In my dreams,
Across the barren wastes of beauty,,
When I am far away,
My need it is to come, Oh so close,
Yet when I come near, the vast nest I touch,
And that which is Dartmoor does swallow my being,

Feel Rock of Granite carved by wind, alone,
On Tors ever stretching into those glorious Heavens,
Listen to those babbling brooks,
Smell purple heather, yellow gorse
See dark wooded glade of green,

Moody is the magic of a Dartmoor scene,
Moments of Sun, and chill-en winds,
Together with Snows so deep,
Mists which fade in, blotting out,
Animals live upon a Dartmoor scene,
Stag noble head aloft,
Fox cunning cat like, the lone hunter in all pursuits,
Then come Bader Otter, Hare and Squirrel,
Black face sheep and Moorland Cattle,
Forgetting not, that which is part of a Dartmoor Scene,
Ponies,
Magpie; nature great collector share the skies with
Hawk and Falcon,

With all these creatures who share the Moor,
There is another, Mankind,
Dartmoor Man called it,
Or did it call Man?
Casting spells over them who came,
Who first love the magic of a Dartmoor scene?
For a cruel love it is, a love so deep in depth of mood,
Men have died loving it,
Those who come in Summer searching out the know not what!
Leave, having found it not!
Return they must to find the Magic of a Dartmoor Scene,

Oh, my words are few and futile,
I cannot express my feelings for Dartmoor and her Moods,
Paper is a man made medium,
To hold in the hand,
And Dartmoor is living,
And therefore cannot be held in the hand.

Written Lydford Church Yard
1982

MINE EYES TO SEA

Mine eyes to Sea, O Lord,
Here I sit, quiet, alone, well almost alone,
Listening semi-consciously to the winds four that howl,
And Sea which roar, with foaming white crests of spray,
The Sun is shining at me with that Ghostly grin
As if to say, I'll be back once more my friend. just wait and see,
For we are in the longest of all British Seasons, Winter cold and bleak,
Though Christmas has gone before,
So the joys of Spring cannot be far away,
These are the things that mine eyes to see, O Lord,

'Tis now that locals as myself
Wander the Golden Coast, and tread these glistening sands,
Wrapped up warm, with scarves a-drooping,
Noses red, ears a funny shade of blue,
And eyes a- weeping with the cold,
We wander, stopping momentarily to stare at Lundy
As generations before have done,
An Isle full of Magic and mystery.
When Sun is hot, again my Friend,
The shall Folks come from afar,
To bathe again upon these Golden Coasts, O Lord.
Charles Kingsley's Westward ho!
                                                  I see,

Hartland Point, I do spy,

With its light,
As I taste, taste the Salt upon my tongue,
Henry Williamson's famous two rivers, continually bid adieu

Adieu,

And I wave a sad farewell.
To Tarka,
For somewhere beyond mine eyes my friend,
Is another Shore,
Where Gods mighty, Mighty, Seas do Roar.

Saunton Sands
1981

CATARACT

Waterfall!

TAW BOY

Taw Boy,
Mischievous of Play,
Elements,
Of Soldiers,
Brothers,
Flow on Flow,
When the Salmon were seen to
Of leapt up Stream,

From your Granite Tors,
Was a Birth,
Breach,
Carving out your Flow,

Then came School,
You old Deceiver,
Estuary Flow,
Was Work,
Time,
Tarka Time,
First with Timber,
Then at Pages,
Turning a Library of Pages,

He has travelled,
Moor on Moor,
Spells those Words,
Silver in their Flow,
You Socialist Rebel,

Holding tight to your Quill,

Flow on Flow,
From your Granite Birth,
A seed,
That thin Blue Line,

Now Estuary Flows,
Chiming now,
Running from Moor to Dune,
Were two hearts first entwine,
Telling of Two Seasons Story,
Is this the Purple Heather,
Long since washed,
When a Piano Played,
Big Ted was Mad,
And Growled so,

When our Deer were running,
Bloody,
Such when was told,
Ore on Ore,
Of your Granite Birth,

For told when Sung,
By the Thatcher's Green Cockade,
Lost in haze of distant Sun,
Was this Delicate ways,

Is this Child,
Now in Middle age,

Walks in Leaves,
Speaking well,
Of Maroons blown,
From Sands of Faded Youth,
You Tidal Waters Rise,
Granite Moon,
Oh cast that Shadow,
Waning Ear!

                                              Autobiographical

MEN AT THEIR BENCHES

Fathers and Sons,
Fathers and Sons,

Have worked at their benches,
Have worked at their benches,

Beside our river that flows,
Beside our river that flows,

Under the Arches and out to the Seas,
Under the Arches and out to the Seas,

Listenin; for the hooter that blows,
Listenin; for the hooter that blows,

Grey is hair,
And Grey the face,
In this tidal monotony,

Knowing his day,
Spires and Towers will beckon,
                Will beckon,

Fathers and Sons,
Fathers and Sons,

Beside our river that flows,
Beside our river that flows,

Under the Arches and out to the Seas,
Under the Arches and out to the Seas,

Deceiving both,

Men their Benches,

Collecting Time and their Watches,
Time and their Watches.

>Written in memory of those at
>Shapland & Petters
>My Time 1979 – 85

THE OLD WORKS HOOTER

When The Old Hooter Blew,
In Those Far Off Days,
Good Days,
Were They,
There Was A Mass Exodus,
From The Old Works,

For The Workers Would Run,
Or Cycle,
Streaming At Speed,
Across The Long Bridge,
Toward Freedom,
And The Town,

There Towns Folk Could Set Their Time Pieces,
On The Old Works Hooter,
Regular,
Carried By The Wind,
And Time And Tide,
Were The Ears Of The Gulls,
Was The Time And Age Of The Town,
                              Flowing,

Under The Arches,
And Out To The Seas,

Anyway The Old Works Hooter,
Was More Faithful,
And Reliable Than The Towns Four Faced Deceiver,

Standing There in The Middle Of The Square!

> The Shapland & Petters
> Work Hooter

MY WIRELESS

My Wireless Is,
The Imagination,
Of The Greater Pallet,

    Painted!

WORTHY FARM
(Pilton)

Somer People,
Glastonbury,

Wearied 'n' wonderful,
Wearied 'n' wonderful,
Where Rainbows aren't illusions,
           Aren't illusions,

Folks,
Down on the Farm,
Down on the Farm,
Michael Milks,
Milks,
His Methodist religion,
Between Clay, Cider, 'n' Stars,
           Cider, 'n' Stars,

Aquarius has come,
With the Rain,
The Mud,
And the Shit,
Rides King Arthur,
And Christ Himself,
Along the Mystic trail,
Of Purple Colour,
And fantasy,
When at Play,

Hash is taken,
Taken,
When,
Swallows your L.S.D.
A Pill to Pop,
Goes the Weasel,

Down on the Farm,
Down on the Farm,
They're Rocking,
They're Rocking,

To the Pyramid Tune,
To the Pyramid Tune.

FLOWERS

I Talked To The Flowers,
               Then,

Although I Knew The Flowers,
         Would Actually Die,
Then,

With Your Summers
         Longing,

A Sweet Perfume Made,
             Then,

In Golden Bands!

SATAN'S APPROACH

Solemnly,
Solemnly,

I went to the Beach,
Down to the Beach,
Tangled in its Weed,
Where the Crows Nests are,
In Dereliction,
In Dereliction,
To Stir the Waters,
Grey,
And Green,
Dragging My Chains,

Was this Lame Man Walking,
Lost in the Swim,
Broad Foot,
And Crow Foot,
The Gulls Squawked,

Loosing My Innocence's,
For Satan had greeted Me,
That Same Morning,
Beguiling and Smiling,
Sifting Me in Winters Approach,
Dragging My Chains Behind,
Dragging My Chains Behind,
Captivating like Some Magician,
                        Or Prince,

Conjuring,
Running on the Tide,
Time and Tide,
Riding his Great Leviathan,
In Worlds of Aching Groaning Mists,
           He Was to Laugh,
                    Laugh!!

Humorously,
PWUCKING Man's Desire,
Of Lie and Hate,
Pure Hate!
Making Waves,
      Waves,

Full of Face,
Was The Clown,
Was The Clown!

ROSE HILL CHILDREN'S HOSPITAL

Purple Pain,
Barbed 'n' torn,
Flowers unlike a band-aid,
With crutch 'n' cast,
Running deep,
Like blood,
Through empty canyons,
Of my mind,
Mind and tears,

Spilling tears,
Like a cloud,
On a rain soaked lawn,
When a brother was born,
When a brother was born,

When comes the Ebony Face,
First of a kind,
To Smile,
Round and Dark,
Full of Face,
Was that Caribbean Sun,
Full of Promise,

Now the boy is walking,
Tasting bitter herbs,
Along that Rhododendron path,
When crucified,
Like a Christ Child,

In the Night,
So Casts,
Separated,
Through the Gaping Window,
Under a Crescent Moon,
Of,
Purple Pain,
      Pain!

Granddad came Walking.

                                           Torquay
                              A Childhood Memory

THE CHILDREN'S WARD

Crutches 'n' Sticks,
Chair Of My Chair,
And Wheels,
For Our World,

Is There Abuse Here?
When Long White Coats Mix,
With Dark Commonwealth Nurses,
And Physio Terrorists,

Is This Some Kind Of Kicking Shed?
For Those Who Have C.P.
With Plasters,
And Calipers Of Iron,
Weighed 'n' Stretched On Traction,
                              Like Me,

Is This Some Kind Of Kicking Shed?
A Window To A World,
Of Screaming Kids,
And Pain,

Of Heart Dancing,
When Parents Leave,
Spilling Tears Over,
Wrinkles To A Life,
When Spoken In Dreams,
                          Madonna!

CHILDREN OF THE TERRACE
(Memories Of Cleave Terrace 62-63)

Keith And Caroline,
Lived In The Terrace,
Lived In The Terrace,
And Played In The Road,
Played In The Road,
With Wheels And Carts,
They Played In The Road,
Played In The Road,

Being The Kids From The Garage,
Going Ever Faster,
To Meet Their Future,
To Meet Their Future,
With Their Wheels That Spun,
Wheels That Spun,
Did The Kids From The Garage,

Being Sun Drenched,
Freckled And Fair,
Freckled And Fair,
Without A Care,
Were The Kids From The Garage,
For As For I,
I Knew Them Well,
With Their Toys,
And Without A Care,

Were The Kids From The Garage,

With Wheels That Spun,
Wheel That Spun,
Going Ever Faster,
To Meet Their Future,
To Meet Their Future,
Beneath That Sun Drenched Terrace,
Of Childhood Play,
Of Yesterday,
Of Yesterday,

When That Life We Lead,
Was Worth Living So,
And Nothing But An Adventure Then,
Of Wheels And Carts,
Wheels And Carts!

TURNING DAYS

Turning Leaves,
A bit Like Turning Pages,
Those Printers are Setting,
Casing them All,
For Old Keppie Has Been At Work,
Ready For The Morrows Dead Line,
Anyway Autumn Coloured Leaves,
Come Wednesday,
Melancholic,
Blustery Like Tuesday,

Wednesday In Queen Street,
Shops Are Closed,
Like The High Street,
Use To Be,
Family Business All,
Like Magg's,
Of This Septic Isle,

For Tomorrow May Come,
With The Dawning,
Of Our Tide,
Also With The Red Sky,
Haunting Those Of All Hallows,
For My Lord Is My Protector,
And Watches Over Me,
Allowing Me To Awake,
If I Should Be So Lucky?
                        Lucky!

THE CENTRAL BELT

The Central Belt,
Of Scotland,
Can Certainly Walk The Walk,
And Talk The Talk,
Of Sectarianism,
Lost In Its Grey,
Of Stadiums,
Of Play,
Between The Sticks,
And The Bulging Nets,
Again,
Again,
Of Bloodline,
And Song.
Bloodline,
And Song!

Written Whilst In Motherwell Scotland
1992

89

I Don't Know What It Is Like,
To Taste The Word,
With My Skin,
Other Than To Get Lost,
In The Arms Of The Female,
Before Me,
In Half Light,
Of Summers Haze,
Catching Her Back,
Through The Nets Of the Shaded Room,
Stands My Opposite Form,
There With Open Arms,
Crowned By Rays Of Sunlight,
Then I am Toughed!

Summer 1989

BRUSH STROKES

He Who Paints A Portrait,
Captures A Most Distant Image,
 Through The Eye,

Through The Eye,
Of Heavenly Tranquillity!

THE BLUE PLANET
(A Thought For COP 27 - Egypt 22)

Its Our Home,
You Know,
    Folks,

Spinning,
Spinning,
Travelling In Orbit,

Starving,
And Warring,
With Brother Against Brother,
For Can We Save Our Home?
If We Work As One,

Or Are We Meant To Save It,
                At all?

For Once There Was a Man,
That Came And said,
Heaven And Earth Shall Pass Away,
But My Word Shall Not Pass Away,

So Then Folks,
The Question is,
Greta,

Are We Really Set To Save This
Spinning Orbiting Globe?

That We Call Home,
Rotating In The Darkness,
           Of Space,

Against The Fingering Thumb,
        Of God Our Father!

AUTUMNS MILL SIDE WANDER

The Fish Leaped,
The King Fishers Dived,
The Deer Appeared,
As Did The Fox,
And The Badger Played,
The Other Side Of The Stream,
For The Wild Wood was Alive
      With Life Abundant,

Together With The Laughing Giggling Stream,
Carrying Its Ores,
And Speaking Of Fortune,
With Its Fragrant Wass Water,
              Tasting,

Running True To Time,
By Side Of The Old Well,
As The Squirrel Gathered Nuts,
For His Season,

For The Litchen Grew,
And The Air Must Have Been Pure There,
Long Since Time Ago,
When I would Wander,
Beneath The Ole Bridge.
Of Autumn's Fungi-Told,
Just As The Folklore I Had Once Heard,
                      Then,

Of Thatching Tales,
So Speak Quietly Now,
Together With Those Whispering Trees,
Beside The Old Mill,
Left Over Of Fortune,
Like The Bridge,
We Had Crossed,
Appearing!

A Lydford Wander

BEYOND THE SALLOW TREE
(A Christmas Carol)

When Tambourine And Carols,
With Hushed And Still Voices,
Did Sound This Way,
The Pavement Artist Did Weep,
                     This Way,

For Warm Drinks Were Handed Out,
When Society Spoke This Way,
Doing Their Charity,
The War Cry Was Handed Out,
Scribbling Graffiti,
Beneath The Lights Of A Christmas
                            Tree,

For We Have More in Common,
Than We Do Apart,
When Society Spoke This Away,
Beyond The Sallow Tree,
With Knives And Crime,
There Would Be A Death That Came,

Beyond The Sallow Tree,
To Share,
Was The Son,
A Death To Share,

For We Have More In Common,
Than We Do Apart,

When Glows Winters Sallow Ball,
At That Eastern Inn,
Where There Was No Room,
Peter Went Forth To Tell His Lords Story,
Beyond The Sallow Tee!

LAMENT ON MARCH 27TH

Looking At Me.
Through Windows Of Eyes Of Blue,

And Fair,

Was The Fawn Of The Forest,
In The Seventeenth Years Of His Passing,
                                          Now,

Grief Is A Strange Beast,
All Hung Over Of Wounds,
                Tattooed!

A POEM FOR MOTHERING SUNDAY

My Niece Is A Woman Now,

    A Mother,

There's Nothing Better To Be,

    See Them Inter Act.

MOURNING SCENE

Well Things Like This,
Don't Usually Happen
                Here,

Yet It Has,
    It Has,

To Our Morning Scene,
Caught On Camera,
When White Are The Faces
                Like Stone,

Silent Stunned,
For A Child Is Now Dead,
And Mourning Scene,
                Weeps,

A Tearful Good Bye,
Between The Police,
And Their Ribbons,

Coloured Balloons Are Life,
Like Prayer Cards Of Old Ascend,
With Your Teddy Bears And Toys,

And Blood Is Hosed From Our Day,
In Mourning Scene,
Though Not Alas A Fading Memory!!

THE BLACK MADONNA

Crystal streams run,
Silver in their Fortune
With Alpine hurt,
When,
Ripples the Wind,
Song,
For Black is the Face,
Of our Lady Madonna,
           Sweet,

Does She Weep,
Tears,
Behind Her Bars,
Those wretched Bars,
In our begotten Chapel,
Of the Mountain,
           Far,

For a King has lost his Crown,
           Lost his Crown,

Oh Ebony wood,
Smile on me Michael!

           At The Church Of Częstochowa

ALBATROSS

I am A Child,
On A Beach,
That Is Scared Of The Sand Man,
With Shells To My Ears,
    Shells To My Ears,

I am A Child,
On A Beach,
That Has A Vivid Imagination,
Spilling Over,
Spilling Over Of Play,

I am A Child,
On A Beach,
Where The Coloured Huts Rest,
Watching The Shore,
For Ones Journey Is There,
              There,

And Far Away,
And Far Away,
With The Saling

        Albatross,
        Albatross,

Oh Whisper It Now,
        Now!!

STREET DEATH

Street Death,
Sudden Death,
Aimless Death,
Pointless Death,
Outside The Old Rose Crown,

Glass Death,
Stabbing Death,
Murderous Death,
Dark Death,
There's Blood On The Floor,

Street Death,
And a Mother Cries,
Knowing She Will Never Get Over It,
Only Turn A Corner!!

PICTURES AND PAINTINGS
(A Muse)

People Always Want,
Pictures And Paintings,
However Abstract,
Rather Than Words,
Dear Priceless Words,
Passing As Blood,
That Write Themselves,

For I Have A Silver Nib,
A Silver Nib,
Running Through My Veins,
          Musing,
          Musing,

On Ventures Told,
And When?
Without Think Of Summers,
Like a Love Affair,
My Dear,
Lying Beneath Those Stolen,
Stolen,
    Stars Of Ours,

Repeats The Ancients!!

BEDOWIN'S A PEOPLE BEYOND
(A Memory in the wilderness, 90
Or Lost In A Moment)

Through The Marriage Of The Heat Haze,
                         We See them,

Appearing To Be Godless,
Knowing Their Truth,
Beneath The Compass Of Dark Sky
                 Stars That Fall,

Civilization Cannot Hold Them,
As They Greet Us,
Being Bound To Wander,
Tied To Their Desert Floor,
With Caravan Of Camel, Mule,
               And Goat,

Their Days Stagger From One To The Other,
Being Broad Foot,
And Club Foot,
Their Gate Wanders For Hole To Hole,
Under Know Bodies Command,
Was There A Boundary Man

A People' Seemingly Lost,
To An Ages When,
Memories When-

With Children At Play,

With An Old TV,
Women Are Busy,
Out Of Sight,
Beneath The Canvas,

Although Amid The Calling,
Its A Men Only Society,
And Dangerous For The Likes Of Us,

Surrounded By Bedowin Males,
Westerners As We Are,
Eager As They Saw fit,
To Buy The Pretty Yellow Haired Woman,
Standing Lost In The Middle Of Our Party,
Not Knowing Where To Look,
Trying To Advert Her Eyes,
From Their Black Like Hawk Like Ones,
Of Jagged Teeth,
And Cheerful Laughter,

The Cost They Were Clamouring For
Was A Good Price,
As They Saw It,
That Of Two Hundred Of The Best Camels!

For The Winds And The Sand Man,
Took Them,
Spirited Them,
From View!

CLEAVE TERRACE

Blue was our door,
When character those places had,
Long time since,
During days of yore,
The way to Life,
Was our stained floor,
Yellow Selling,
Creaking Stairs,
Together with rattling Windows,
        And greying hairs,

Gulls squawked at Chimney tops,
High 'n' away from the Bay,
When Tit Birds pecked at Milk bottle tops,
Golden in colour,
Down amid the Terrace,
Where Automobiles drove,
And Keith and Caroline played in their Street,
Dragging their Cart way from the Hill,
For it happened to be the Tuesday,
After bank holiday Monday,
And the Kids would soon be back at School,
        Conkers 'n' all,
During darker Evenings.

The Women opened the Crown,
For Chapel was done,
Just as the Boy sat with his Bear,
The Policeman was their,

Doing his duty,
That September Morn,
When the Frosts sat in their Garden,
Along came Godfrey wearing that Hat!
In Stately in procession,
Sitting down with the Boy,
As the Swallows would Fly home to the Sun,
                        The South African Sun.

MR. NICHOLAS OUR GEOGRAPHY TEACHER

Oh Our Geography Teacher,
Had Long Hair,
And A Beard,
With His Open Toed Sandals,
And Beads,
To Match
Looking As He Did A Bit Like
      Jesus,

For He Lived On A Farm,
And Smelt Of The Sheep,
And Goats,
For We Respected Him,
Our Geography Teacher,
   Mr. Nicholas,

For He Took Us On Trips,
And Taught Us Of The America's,
Scratching The Board,
And Waking Us Up,
With His Chalk,
So White,
With One Awful Fright,
Was He Jesus?
 We Asked,

Having Come, To Judge, Us,
In His Wretched Class,
Of Seventy Two!

POINT OF CONTACT

Oh I've Got A Wardrobe,
A Wonderful Wardrobe,
Of Old Shoes,
All Beat Up,
That I Don't Use,
Black Shoes,
And Blue Shoes,
Coloured Shoes,
And Differing Trainers,

Oh I've Got A Wardrobe,
A Wonderful Wardrobe,
Of Old Shoes,
And I'm Not Throwing Them Out,
For They Are My Old Shoes,
For They In Turn Are My Point Of Contact,
With Gods Good Earth,

Feel It,
Adams Soil,
Beneath You,
Quake With Its Birth
          Pangs!

COMING HOME
(The Empty Church)

I Came Home,
To Find You Weren't
      There,

Amid Your Christian Songs,
      And Prayer,

That All Was Cool,
And Grown,
And Empty
    There,

That Jesu's Love,
Had Gone From There,
For The Vicars Words Rang Oh So Hollow
      Over There,

Amid Its Wealth,
And Glistening Spire,
The Rooter He Seemed So Proud,
Rotating In The Wind,

For The Church Did Hide Behind,
Its Frantic Dairy Of Evangelical Business Events,
      There,

Locking Out The Dear Good Lord,
To Share,

Whilst Reader In The Park,
  Just Over There!

A Tale Of Woe

HISTORY AVENUE

We Are All The People Of The Past,
In History Avenue,
                  Just At Another Point!

GOLD DUST

Bring Things To End,
And Turning Them To Memory,
Is But Gold Dust,
        Folks!

FAREWELL

I Love This Time Of Year,
With Autumn Mellow,
Fragrant,
In Her Moisture,
She Is At Peace,
For Darkness,
And Winters Approach,

Everything Changes,
Kind Of Slow,
The Atmosphere Is,
Oh Well On The Cooler Side,
Of Fungi,
And Moss,

My Darling,
Beneath Your Coloured Canopy,
Of Colour,
In Their Wistful Wane,
Of A Blazing Rage,
    Of Farewell!

FULL STOP

THE STORM,
will END.

POST

We Are,
       Post, Empire,

We Are,
       Post, Windrush,

We Are,
       Post. Kennedy,

We Are,
       Post, The Beatles,

We Are,
       Post, Apollo,

We Are,
       Post, Nam.

We Are,
       Post, The Winter Of Discontent,

We Are,
       Post, The Miners Strike,

We, Are,
       Post, Jubilee,

We Are,
       Post, Floyd,

We Are,
        Post, Brexit,

We Are,
        Post, Covid,

We Are,
        Post, Elizabeth The Second.

Printed in Great Britain
by Amazon